LET'S WALK THERE!
Series Editor: Bruce Bedford

Eastern England

Hilary Bradt

*Line drawings by
David Wasley*

JAVELIN BOOKS
POOLE · NEW YORK · SYDNEY

MARKET RASEN ①

② MABLETHORPE

③

● Lincoln

LINCOLNSHIRE

● BOSTON

⑧ ● CROMER

⑨

● KING'S LYNN

● GRANTHAM

NORWICH ● ⑩

GREAT YARMOUTH

④ NORFOLK

⑤ ● PETERBOROUGH ⑪ LOWESTOFT

⑫

⑬

ELY ● ⑥ SUFFOLK

CAMBRIDGESHIRE ALDEBURGH ●

CAMBRIDGE BURY ST EDMUNDS ⑭ ⑮

⑦ ⑯ IPSWICH WOODBRIDGE

⑰

⑱

CONTENTS

First published in the UK 1987 by Javelin Books,
Link House, West Street, Poole, Dorset, BH15 1LL

Copyright © 1987 Javelin Books

Distributed in Australia by
Capricorn Link (Australia) Pty Ltd,
PO Box 665, Lane Cove, NSW 2066

British Library Cataloguing in Publication Data

Brandt, Hilary
    Eastern England. —(Let's walk there)
    1. Walking — England — Guide-books
    2. England — Description and travel — 1971-
    — Guide-books
    I. Title   II. Series
    914.26′04858   DA650
        ISBN 0 7137 1771 8

Cartography by Ron Rigby
Cover picture:
Kentwell Hall courtesy of The British Tourist
Authority, Britain on View (BTA/ETB)

Typeset by Inforum Ltd, Portsmouth
Printed in Great Britain by Cox & Wyman Ltd, Reading, Berks.

INTRODUCTION

As worthwhile as any walk might be, it becomes doubly appealing if it takes you to some place of special interest. The nine books in this series, covering England, Scotland and Wales were conceived to describe just such walks.

A full description of the walk's objective is given at the start of each chapter. The objectives are diverse, giving a wide choice. Most are non-seasonal, and involve little walking in themselves once you are there.

Following the description of the objective, each section of the walk is clearly described, and a specially drawn map makes route-finding straightforward. As well as detailing the route, the authors describe many subsidiary points of interest encountered along the way.

The walks are varied and most are easy to follow. None of them is too taxing, except in the severest weather. Most are circular, returning you to your car at the starting point; half the walks in this volume are accessible by public transport. Family walkers with young children will find plenty of shorter routes to suit their particular needs, whilst those with longer legs can select from more substantial walks.

Readers will certainly increase the enjoyment which they and others derive from the walks if they respect the countryside by following the Country Code.

Bruce Bedford
Series Editor

ACKNOWLEDGEMENTS

The walks in this book were selected with the generous help of numerous people. Members of the Ramblers' Association provided much information and advice; I am particularly grateful to John Andrews (Suffolk), and Major Brett Collier (Lincolnshire). Two county councils (of the four contacted) provided exceptional help – Suffolk and Lincolnshire, with the latter deserving congratulations for their energetic campaign to re-establish neglected footpaths; my special thanks to Ray Taylor, Helen Brooks and Peter White.

Also deserving special mention are Albert Simmonds, who painstakingly located numerous Suffolk newspaper cuttings, Deborah Ardizzowe who provided the Blythburgh walk, Gerald Nason of Laxfield, Noel Farnsworth of Alford, Stephen Lloyd of Cambridge, Peter Evans of Ely, Riki Dearden of Cley, M.J. Bradley of Nene Park, and the Morrisons of Woodbridge.

Hilary Bradt

Walk 1
NORMANBY LE WOLD AND TEALBY
LINCOLNSHIRE
6½ or 4½ miles

The *by* endings of many local place names here show their Danish origin so it is fitting that this walk to Lincolnshire's highest 'village' (hamlet would be closer) should be partly along the Viking Way, the county's long-distance footpath. The Lincolnshire Wolds, a designated Area of Outstanding Natural Beauty, are chalk hills rising rather suddenly from the surrounding flatness and providing spectacular views. It is for these views that I have chosen Normanby as the destination, so save this walk for a clear day.

Walesby lies to the east of the A46 Lincoln to Grimsby road, a few miles from Market Rasen. Park on Moor Road near The Red House where there is room for several cars on the verge. You will see the Viking Way signposted up a well-used track. This takes you to a fork in the path beyond a cattle grid where you turn left. After a concrete bridge the track starts to rise steeply as you approach a seemingly near-vertical hillside ahead. A finger post, however, marks a fork in the path and by turning left you avoid the climb and contour round the hill following the hedge/fence. Beyond a stile and gate is a farm track which leads to the surfaced access road for Claxby House Farm. Go right here and join Park Road which leads to Claxby village.

Claxby church can be reached via a 'courtesy path' leading straight ahead where the road makes a right-angled turn. The charming ironstone church has some old gravestones – one dated 1765 – and a 1595 monument inside. Particularly

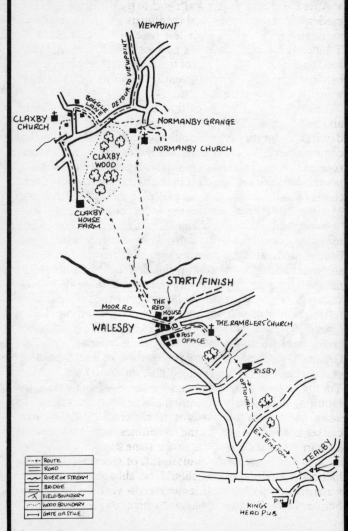

NORMANBY LE WOLD

1 mile

VIEWPOINT

BOGGY LANE M.W.

DETOUR TO VIEWPOINT

CLAXBY CHURCH

NORMANBY GRANGE

NORMANBY CHURCH

CLAXBY WOOD

CLAXBY HOUSE FARM

START/FINISH

MOOR RD

THE RED HOUSE

WALESBY

THE RAMBLERS' CHURCH

POST OFFICE

RISBY

OPTIONAL EXTENSION

TEALBY

KINGS HEAD PUB

P.H.

	ROUTE
	ROAD
	RIVER OR STREAM
	BRIDGE
	FIELD BOUNDARY
	WOOD BOUNDARY
	GATE OR STILE

interesting, however, is the figure above the chancel arch of a man evidently suffering from severe toothache. There is a similar one in the Normanby church.

After the church the footpath goes to the right, skirting the garden of Claxby House, and then turns left into a field and joins Mulberry Road. Turn left here and then right at a T-junction along Boggle Lane past some attractive old brick and stone houses. At the end of this land a footpath continues between a hedge and fence, eventually joining a gravel drive which leads to Normanby Rise.

Your route continues uphill to the top of Claxby Wood, and then right along a footpath. However, if it is a very clear day it is worth making a detour to the highest point in the county; keep climbing up the steep road and take the first turning to the left and continue to the top of the hill. The high point is a couple of fields over to the right (547 feet) but from the road you may be able to pick out the towers of York Minster and Selby Abbey to the north.

Return to the footpath that runs by the wood. The humpy meadow on your left shows the Wolds at their most flamboyant; underneath the chalky soil are layers of clay, sandstone and ironstone, pushed up and moulded by the forces of nature. Unsuitable for cultivation, these miniature hills and valleys have for centuries provided pasture for animals and a haven for wild flowers.

At the end of the woods bear left, away from the fence, and climb towards a stile to the left of the farm, Normanby Grange. On reaching the road turn right to Normanby church, beautifully located on the edge of the escarpment. Your route, the Viking Way, goes to the right of the church, following the escarpment along the edge of two large fields – where you get the best views of the walk: on a clear day you can see Lincoln Cathedral, and sometimes Boston Stump – to a smart new stile. Continue in the same direction until you cross a stile into grassland often full of sheep. If you look half-right from here you should be able to see the next waymark on a pole that guides you across a marshy area at the bottom of the hill and diagonally up the other side. You

'The Ramblers' Window', All Saints Church, Walesby

10

should now be able to see the finger post that marked the division of the path at the beginning of the walk and can follow the track back to the road and the parking place.

There is no pub in Walesby and since Tealby has a particularly pleasant one it is well worth walking on to this village which many people consider the most attractive in the Wolds. If someone can meet you there with the car, so much the better. The path to Tealby is the continuation of the Viking Way and passes the most appealing church in the area, popularly known as The Ramblers' Church.

Turn left at the road where you left your car and walk through the village, taking the short road to the right that leads to the Post Office. Turn left and take the waymarked track at the end of the road which leads up to All Saints Church. It is a steep climb but well worth it, even if you are not going on to Tealby, for the views and for the rural charm of the church. (A note in the porch warns visitors to keep the door closed to prevent sheep from wandering inside). The Hikers' Window, showing Christ with a group of Sunday walkers, was donated by the Lincolnshire Ramblers Association in 1951, and a special ramblers service is held on Trinity Sunday each year.

The Viking Way continues through a gate opposite the church porch, and takes you over two stiles to a dramatically steep hillside which you follow down to the left, across a stream, and up the other side towards Risby Manor Farm. Cross the track leading to the farm and continue following the Viking Way signs past Castle Farm (on your right) to Tealby. The Kings Head, a fourteenth-century pub with a thatched roof, makes a perfect end to the walk.

Walk 2
ALFORD FOLK MUSEUM
& WINDMILL
LINCOLNSHIRE
7 or 5 miles

The market town of Alford, at the foot of the Lincolnshire
Wolds, has two places of especial interest which together
make a fine objective for a walk. The Folk Museum (open
Monday to Friday from May to September, 10.30am to 1pm,
and 2pm to 4.30pm) is housed in the thatched Tudor Manor
House. Dating from 1540, this was once a timbered building
but it was bricked around in 1661. Apart from displays on
local archaeology, transport and agriculture, the museum
depicts scenes from the nineteenth century, including a vet's
surgery, a cobbler's shop, a chemist's shop and a sweet
maker.

Alford Mill is occasionally open to the public (between
12pm and 6pm on bank holidays from Easter to August, and
on the third Saturday in July and August). Even if closed, it is
a fine working windmill and worth a look. Alford also has a
weekly craft market on Fridays (from June to the end of
September), and an August Bank Holiday Fair.

Begin the walk at Rigsby, to the west of Alford, where
there is ample parking on the verge. Just beyond Rigsby
House Farm is a well marked public footpath leading to the
right down a clear track towards Ailby Wood Farm. This
track loops around a small wood, crosses the old railway and
arrives at a road. Continue following the footpath on the
other side of the road, over a stile and by a fence and dyke on
the path's left.

When you reach a gap in this fence cross into the adjacent

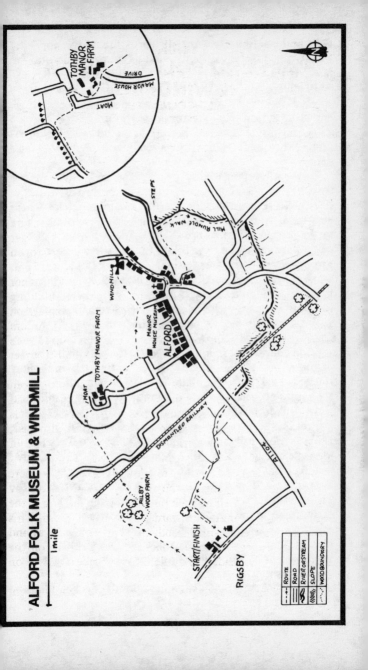

ALFORD FOLK MUSEUM & WINDMILL

1 mile

TOTHBY MANOR FARM

MANOR HOUSE DRIVE

MOAT

N

STEPS

MILL RUNGDITCH WALK

WINDMILL

TOTHBY MANOR FARM

MANOR HOUSE MUSEUM

ALFORD

MOAT

DISMANTLED RAILWAY

A1104

AILBY WOOD FARM

START/FINISH

RIGSBY

	ROUTE
	ROAD
	RIVER OR STREAM
	SLOPE
	WOOD BOUNDARY

field and continue towards a stile in the hedge opposite. Follow the edge of the field round to your left and into the next field. Leave the hedge and dyke when they turn left and walk towards the right-hand corner of Tothby Manor Farm's moat. Follow the waymarks left and then right over a bridge and stile and diagonally across the farm grounds towards a gate. Stay inside the fence, however, and follow it as it curves around the buildings and brings you out on the manor house drive.

Under a weeping willow on the lawn of Tothby Manor (private) is a plague stone which formerly stood at the Rigsby-Well crossroads on the Alford-Spilsby road, where provisions were left for the sufferers of this epidemic which killed 132 people in Alford.

To continue to the town follow the drive to a footpath sign through a gate on your left. At the corner of the field is another gate and a good track to the next field where you bear right to a concrete bridge across the dyke. Cross this and follow the track towards a kissing gate backed by a lamp and with the church steeple behind. This will take you to Park Lane which leads to the Manor House Museum, but you may want to continue through the fields to the windmill. Instead of going through the gate to Park Lane, turn left and follow the well-used footpath to East Street. The windmill is just to the right. To reach the town centre, from the windmill turn right and simply follow the A1104.

From the centre of town you can follow the A1104 back towards the Rigsby road or join the Mill Rundle Walk for the longer excursion. The Mill Rundle was once one of three watercourses draining the land around Alford. Because of the danger of flooding it was decided to dig a new channel for the Mill Rundle and purchase an additional strip of land beside the watercourse as access for maintenance workers. The land owners and Drainage Board were later persuaded to allow this footpath to be used by ramblers. This popular path is easy to follow and interesting for the birds, plants and butterflies that flourish by the edge of the water.

Start at the church and follow South Market Place to

Alford Mill

Caroline Street. The Mill Rundle Walk is signposted. Follow the track, despite a 'no trespassers' sign, past some waste land of thistles and willowherb (a good place for butterflies) to a flight of concrete steps down to the Mill Rundle channel.

Turn right and follow the bank (the route is well way-marked) to the road which you join at a T-junction. Go straight ahead for a short distance, then right. This section is a dedicated footpath over farmland. The Walk crosses the Mill Rundle and follows its southern bank by a lumpy field headland to the next road where it again crosses the channel. The going is now smoother as you follow the path to the old railway track. Here you turn right by a small copse. The path runs between the railway and the channel, then turns left just before the old Alford station. Follow the hedge then cross the drain by a brick bridge and continue to the road.

Across the A1104 is another footpath sign. The path starts well but used to deteriorate. However, the County Council's plans to waymark and assist in the clearance of this path should be accomplished by now. If you are following a good path give mental thanks to the local Ramblers' Association and to the County Council.

The footpath follows field headlands, crossing various drainage ditches to a spinney where you turn left (ignore the track to the left just before), to emerge eventually on the road by Rigsby church. Take this to the right to return to your starting point.

If churches interest you particularly, before you leave the area it is well worth visiting Marksby, some three miles north-east of Alford. It has a tiny thatched church with box pews and a double-decker pulpit.

Walk 3
TENNYSON COUNTRY:
BAG ENDERBY
LINCOLNSHIRE
6½ or 4½ miles

This part of the Lincolnshire Wolds is strongly associated with Alfred Lord Tennyson, the Victorian poet laureate. Being born and raised here, he probably saw nothing particularly amusing in such place names as Hagworthingham and Bag Enderby (the walk's starting point and objective), plus that nearby rural couple Mavis Enderby and Old Bolingbroke. Surprisingly, there is no Tennyson museum, and the poet's birthplace in Somersby (not on your main route, but worth making the small diversion to for its church and general setting) is not open to the public.

However, there is enough Tennyson memorabilia, and certainly enough fine scenery, to commend this walk through what is considered the most attractive part of the Wolds. The valley owes its beauty to the River Lymn, which provided the inspiration for the poem 'The Brook', so beloved of primary school teachers, and our walk crosses this river several times.

The walk's main objective, Bag Enderby, is a tiny village where Tennyson's father was once rector. In 1879 it was noted that it had a church, three farms, a few cottages, 'while one will look in vain for a house licensed to sell intoxicants'. That description still holds. The fifteenth-century church is built of mouldering green sandstone and nailed to its door is a rusty iron boss from a Saxon shield found in a nearby field. Inside is a map drawn by local schoolchildren which traces the course of Tennyson's brook and all its associations. The treasure of the church is the carved font, depicting familiar

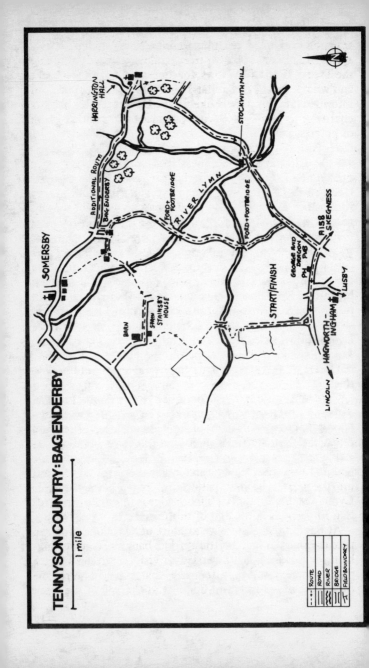

TENNYSON COUNTRY: BAG ENDERBY

1 mile

·-·-·	ROUTE
═══	ROAD
≋≋≋	RIVER
⌐	BRIDGE
⊤	FIELD BOUNDARY

SOMERSBY

HARRINGTON HALL

ADDITIONAL ROUTE

BAG ENDERBY

STOCKWITH MILL

FORD + FOOTBRIDGE

RIVER LYMN

FORD + FOOTBRIDGE

BARN

STAINSBY HOUSE

START/FINISH

GEORGE AND DRAGON PH PUB

A158 SKEGNESS

LINCOLN ← HAGWORTH-INGHAM → LUSBY

and not so familiar religious motifs. These include a hart springing nimbly over two trees while engrossed in licking the Tree of Life which grows, for some reason, from its back, and what seems to be a guitar-strumming saint, though I am informed that this is more likely to be David with his harp. A charming piece of religious art, enhanced by a subtle coating of green algae.

Hagworthingham, where the walk begins, is easily reached via the A158 Lincoln-Skegness road which cuts this once pretty village in two. Approaching from the East, pass the George and Dragon pub on your right and turn up the next road which is marked by a dead-end sign. Park on the slip road (a section of the old road) on your right.

Follow the lane uphill to its end, passing a cottage like a child's drawing with a single enormous chimney, and continue climbing on the footpath to the highest point of the walk. The views in all directions are splendid, and so is the immediate landscape as you follow the footpath down a steep meadow backed by rolling hills with clumps of trees on their shoulders. The brook at the bottom is a tributary of the Lymn. Herons fish here, and Tennyson called the brook's source 'haunts of coot and hern'; the stream is a pleasant reminder of the poem as it runs between ash and willow trees.

Cross the footbridge and continue up the well-marked trail to join a track which leads uphill to more good views then curves round the grounds of Stainsby House. When you reach the farm turn right between the farm buildings. A grassy track takes you downhill and then through a gap in the hedge. Leave the track here and follow the hedge on your left into the next field and down towards some trees and the River Lymn which is crossed via a footbridge leading to a dirt road. Bag Enderby is at the end of this dirt road.

At Bag Enderby you have a choice of directions. You can take the shortest (and prettiest) route back to Hagworthingham, or make a short diversion to visit Tennyson's birthplace, Somersby, via a footpath that runs between the thatched cottage and farm building at the end of the track

Alfred Lord Tennyson

from the river. A third choice, to visit Harrington Hall, is described later.

To walk back to Hagworthingham take the old gravel road from the south-east of the church. This is easy to follow though it may be muddy in parts. It crosses the Lymn via a footbridge and climbs up to a good viewpoint before dropping down to the brook, crossed by another footbridge, after which it becomes the access road to a farm. At the junction of the road to Harrington turn right and continue to the A158 where you turn right to reach your starting point.

From Bag Enderby you can also visit Harrington Hall, although the two mile walk there along the road is not as enjoyable as others in the area. This lovely seventeenth-century manor house is well worth a visit, however, and you can walk back to the car, mainly on roads (see map) via Stockwith Mill, a craft centre and tea room which provides the only refreshments in these parts. Harrington Hall is open on Thursdays from Easter to the end of September, from 2pm to 5pm, and some Sundays through the summer. The garden is open on Wednesdays as well as Thursdays. For further information phone Spilsby (0790) 52281.

Walk 4
STAMFORD
CAMBRIDGESHIRE
8 or 6 miles

The history of Stamford goes back to pre-Roman days when Ancient Britons found the only ford across the River Welland (Stamford means stone ford). Roman settlements gave way to Saxon, the Normans developed and fortified the town, and it grew to prosperity through the cloth trade. There are many royal connections: Queen Boadicea used the ford for hot pursuit of the defeated Ninth Legion; the army that persuaded King John that Magna Carta was a Good Thing assembled in Stamford; and Lord Burghley, whose vast mansion is just outside the town, helped put the first Queen Elizabeth on the throne. The second Queen Elizabeth has been a guest of Burghley's descendants while watching her daughter compete in the annual horse trials.

Today's visitors, seeing the streets of honey-coloured stone buildings, may agree with Sir Walter Scott that Stamford is 'the finest scene between London and Edinburgh'. The old town and St Martins became England's first Conservation Area in 1967; 500 buildings are listed as being of architectural and historical importance.

Uffington, where the walk begins, is a charming small village east of Stamford off the busy A16 to Market Deeping. Stone houses line the road by the church. Park on the verge of Casement Lane by the pub just off the main road. Turn left on the A16 and walk to where the road makes a sharp left-hand turn by the lodge of the former Uffington estate. Note the cheerful stone lions atop the elegant lodge gates.

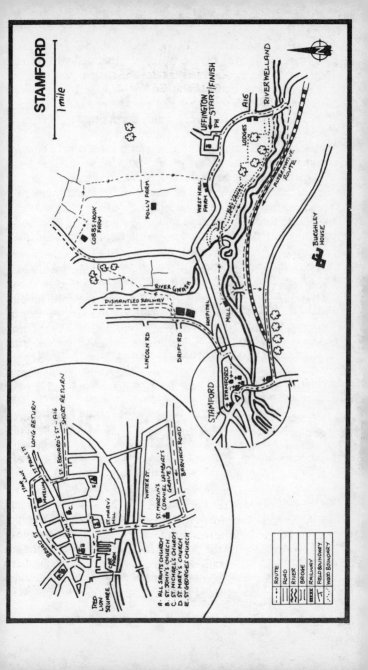

Straight on, a much more tranquil road leads to Barnack, but just before the river bridge turn onto the well-signposted footpath to the right which takes you, without any route-finding problem, into Stamford by following the River Welland. The path sometimes follows close to the river, but more often stays high on the bank bordering the Welland Canal (now dry).

After about a mile of walking you'll meet another path coming in from the right across a bridge. Go over the stile and to the left, keeping the fence on your left, and cross the River Gwash via a footbridge. The spires of St Mary's and All Saints' churches are now visible, as well as other church towers. Ignore another little footbridge across the river and continue to follow its right bank bordering the Welland the field and the track leading to the old water mill.

The shortest way into Stamford is by turning right here, but for the most dramatic entry into the heart of the old town go left, across the river and the railway and along a track to the Barnack Road which borders the Burghley Estate; follow this to the right. In three quarters of a mile you'll find yourself suddenly on High Street St Martins, one of the oldest and architecturally most exciting streets in Stamford.

The following circuit takes you through some of the most attractive streets, but a guidebook or a visit to the Tourist Office on St Mary's Hill will ensure that you miss nothing. The first thing to look at is the grave of Daniel Lambert in St Martin's churchyard. Lambert was the fattest man in England, and when he died in 1809 a wall of his room had to be demolished to remove the body, and twenty men were needed to lower his 32 stone into the grave. St Martin's Church contains the tombs of the Cecil family of Burghley House. Stroll across the river, up St Mary's Hill, examining the church with its lovely spire on the way, and go left to Red Lion Square. Turn right down Broad Street to Stamford Museum (there is also an excellent Brewery Museum on All Saints Street) and on to Star Lane.

Here you must make a decision. The shortest route back to Uffington is to turn right along St Paul's Street and then left

Daniel Lambert, 'the fattest man in England'

25

and left again into St Leonard's Street which leads to Priory Road and the A16. Continue to the water mill and then along the other side of the river where a footpath runs close to the railway line. Alternatively you can vary the walk by taking a newly re-established footpath that runs through water meadows then across farm land to your starting point.

If this latter is your choice, follow St Paul's Street to the hospital and then up Ryhall Road. You will soon escape this dreary part of town by taking the footpath that leads to the right between two corrugated iron fences by the Engineering Works buildings. It runs a short distance down a dismantled railway line before crossing the meadow between pylons to the newly-bridged River Gwash. Continue up the next meadow, with its fine views, to the corner of an enclosed field and on to a stile leading to a lane where there is an interesting old boundary stone.

This lane turns left after a short distance; straight ahead is a green lane. The footpath leads off to the right after about 20 yards, heading to the left of some farm buildings. Because of over-ploughing the path from here, which follows headlands of fields, used to be heavy going, but I hope this will have been rectified by the time you do the walk. If not, take heart: there is some relief on a grassy track before you emerge onto the A16 by West Hall Farm. Turn left to reach your starting point.

Walk 5
NENE VALLEY
CAMBRIDGESHIRE
6 or 4½ miles

Old locomotives, a Roman road, wild flowers and numerous birds, and the beautifully planned and organised Ferry Meadows Country Park are among the pleasures of this valley walk which culminates in a ride on a steam train as the objective.

A well-marked footpath, the Nene Way, follows the course of the Nene river between Wansford Station, the terminus of the Nene Valley Railway, and Ferry Meadows with an extension to Peterborough City Centre. As described, this walk on part of the Nene Way can only be done as a circular route when the trains are running: weekends from April to October, and Tuesdays, Wednesdays and Thursdays during school holidays, plus a few 'Santa Specials' around Christmas. Telephone Stamford (0780) 782854 for details.

Begin at Wansford Station, the headquarters of the Nene Valley Railway, which houses a collection of steam locomotives and carriages from nine countries as well as a railway museum. Just off the A1, eight miles west of Peterborough, it can be reached by car or by steam train (the NVR service was extended to Peterborough in 1986). One of the first trains you'll see at Wansford is 'Thomas', his smiling face instantly recognisable from the Rev. W. Awdry's children's books. This small-power tank engine, built in 1947, was aquired from the British Sugar Corporation and the Rev. Awdry was invited to perform the naming ceremony in 1972. There are also locomotives and carriages from France, Scandinavia and

NENE VALLEY

|——| 1 mile

WANSFORD STATION
START/FINISH

ORDER OF STAMFORD BONNET LINE

ERNINE ST (OLD ROMAN ROAD)

PICNIC AREA

THE NENE WAY

CASTOR BACKWAY

WATER NEWTON

A1

PH

CASTOR

PH

THE NENE WAY

A47

GOLF COURSE

BLUEBELL WOOD

OVERTON LAKE

GUNWADE LAKE

VISITORS CENTRE

FERRY MEADOWS STATION

ALTERNATIVE ROUTE

LYNCH WOODLAND

TO THE A1

B605

CASTOR MILL

BACK DYKE

EASTHOLMES

·-·-·	ROUTE
═══	ROAD
)(	BRIDGE
━━━	THE NENE WAY
≈≈	RIVER
┼┼┼	RAILWAY
ψψψ	REEDS/MARSH

Germany, and a Wagon-Lits restaurant car presented by Thomas Cook Ltd.

Before leaving Wansford, pick up a timetable so you can plan your return from Ferry Meadows by steam train.

The path begins by the railway bridge on the opposite side of the road from the station. Here you will see the symbol of the Nene Way which will be a frequent and welcome reassurance that you are on the correct path. Cross the river and continue close to the railway for half a mile. Look out for the remains of the Stamford branch line, opened in 1869 (the main railway was opened in 1845). A special station for this line had to be built just short of the junction since the management of the two companies could not agree on terms for the use of Wansford station.

After a rather dreary half mile the path leaves the railway and skirts the edge of a field before joining a farm track which is much used by cows and may be muddy. On arriving at the water meadows there is some confusion caused by the track (marked with yellow arrows) that crosses the Nene Way and runs across the river to the village of Water Newton. You should continue along the north bank of the stream known as the Castor Backwater. The reeds here are a favourite haunt of a large variety of water fowl, and there are picnic benches for hungry or weary walkers. Just beyond the picnic area you come to another path junction. Again, ignore the track which crosses the railway and the river and continue to hug the bank by turning right at a fence, crossing a stile, and following the backwater until it meets the main river.

Just after crossing a timber causeway, the path crosses Ermine Street, a Roman road which linked London and Lincoln. The site of what was once a large Roman town, Durobrivae, is to the south, and the straight line of the road north can just be discerned from the Nene Way. Continue to follow the river until you come to a comma-shaped backwater. Here you turn sharp left up a fence (do not continue straight ahead past the 'no fishing' sign) towards a lone lombardy poplar tree and across a little bridge. This takes you up to high ground and you will emerge in Mill Lane.

The age of steam, Nene Valley

There is a gate onto the road, but the official footpath runs to the right, over a stile opposite a copse of poplars, and then left.

Turn right down Mill Lane, past the converted Castor Mill, and bear left at the end onto a particularly lovely stretch of the Nene Way. Shortly after passing the derelict Castor Windmill you cross a small footbridge onto the island (eyot) of East Holmes. This is an excellent area for bird-watching. Another small footbridge (just after the ford used by horse riders) brings you back to the north bank of the river which you follow to the railway, taking time to admire the Lynch Woodland on the opposite bank with its dominant Cedar of Lebanon tree.

At the railway bridge you have a choice. The Nene Way follows the river as it loops round to the north, passing through very attractive meadows and woodland, or you can take the path which crosses the river and follows the railway to Ferry Meadows Station, shortening the walk by a mile and a half.

Continuing along the Nene Way takes you through Ferry Field, ancient common land with some stately trees, and into Bluebell Wood which was once part of Earl Fitzwilliam's estate at Milton Park. Emerging from the woods by the golf course, turn right along a surfaced track and cross the river. Another bridge brings you to Overton Lake, an adventure playground, and all the facilities of Ferry Meadows, including a cafe and very helpful visitor centre.

A few hundred yards down the road is the Ferry Meadows Station, from where you catch the train back to Wansford.

Walk 6
ELY CATHEDRAL
CAMBRIDGESHIRE
3 miles

Ely Cathedral, with its wonderful Norman facade and spacious interior, is justly one of the most famous in Britain. Dating from 1083, the cathedral replaced an earlier religious house founded in 673 by St Etheldreda. The East Anglian princess was so holy she kept her virginity through two marriages but still managed to acquire the land and wealth to establish the Isle of Ely as a major religious centre until the abbey was sacked by the Danes in 870.

In 1323 the original Norman central tower fell down, causing considerable damage to the main fabric of the cathedral. However, this allowed the construction of the Octagon, since called the most daring and original architectural and constructional achievement of the English Middle Ages. The oak beams that support the upper 'lantern' of windows are 63 feet long and three feet thick. Even in those days suitable trees were hard to find and they were brought from all over the kingdom, roads and bridges being specially strengthened for their passage.

The view of Ely Cathedral rising from the flatness of the surrounding fens is one of the most awe-inspiring in England, and the impact is immeasurably greater if this majestic building is approached on foot instead of by car. This short walk is ideal for children (even if they find the cathedral less entrancing than adults) with an abundance of water, hide-and-seek bushes and a railway, and also for natural history enthusiasts since part of the route is along the

ELY CATHEDRAL

¼ mile

	ROUTE
	ROAD
	RIVER
	BRIDGE
	RAILWAY
	GATE OR STYLE
	SLOPE
	REEDS/MARSH
	FENCE

START/FINISH

SUGAR FACTORY

ROSWELL PITS

CUCKOO BRIDGE

ANGLIAN WATER AUTHORITY

RIVER OUSE

SPRINGHEAD LANE

MARKET PLACE

THE VINEYARD

MIDDLE FEN BANK

QUEEN ADELAIDE ROAD

HIGH ST.

CATHEDRAL

CRENELLATED PILLARS

BROAD STREET

CUTTER INN

ELY PARK

STATION

Ely Nature Trail, centred round a group of large ponds which are actually water-filled clay pits. Clay has been dug from this area since the seventeenth century – and perhaps earlier – and used to shore up the river bank. The Roswell Pits are now a haven for waterfowl and other wildlife. A booklet guiding you along the nature trail, with a detailed description of the natural history of the area, can be purchased from the library/Tourist Centre opposite the cathedral.

Your approach for this walk is from the east via Queen Adelaide Way. Watch out for the signpost to Queen Adelaide as you approach Ely on the A142 and park a mile down the road as near as possible to the iron footbridge that crosses the River Ouse on the left. Take the bridge over the river and follow the footpath round to the left through reedy scrub. You'll pass one of the Roswell Pits on the left. There is usually a good selection of water fowl and migratory waders to be seen here, particularly in the spring and autumn.

The footpath now runs rather muddily between black-thorn bushes (and, in the summer, nettles) but soon emerges at a footbridge known as Cuckoo Bridge. Perhaps the many reed buntings and reed warblers, favourite foster parents of the cuckoo, have made this an attractive area for them. Kingfishers are also quite often seen here – look for them perching on the wooden posts at the water's edge, watching for fish. Beyond the bridge are the buildings of the Anglia Water Authority. Pass the Office Stores sign and follow the building round to the left, then hug the fence until you reach a stile into the water meadows. A path takes you to the river edge and then into Ely with lovely views.

Continue following the river, passing under the railway bridge, then under a footbridge to join Quayside leading to The Cutter Inn. Turn right up an alley called Cutter Lane which brings you out on Jubilee Terrace. Walking to the right, along Broad Street, you'll arrive at a handsome pair of crenellated pillars on the left. Through these is Ely Park and a public footpath from which you have an incomparable view of the cathedral. Emerge at Ely Porta, a fourteenth-century

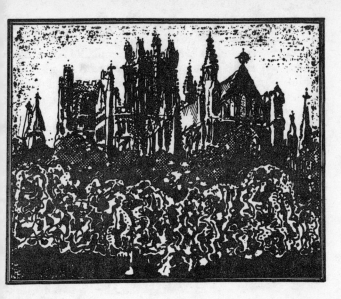

Ely Cathedral

gatehouse, and enter the cathedral just past the Bishop's House on the right.

Give yourself time to stand and stare. The most impressive features are the Octagon and long Norman nave, and also the Lady Chapel. There is a coffee shop in the cathedral and a stained glass museum.

Leave through the Sacrists Gate and turn right down High Street then left into Market Place and on to a street called The Vineyards. There were indeed vineyards in medieval days, belonging to the Bishop of Ely. The road ends in a new housing estate. Turn left and then right and follow a footpath between houses to Springhead Lane. Turn right here, cross the road and take the old lane as it bears round to the left between high and ancient hedges until you emerge at the access road for Anglian Water. Cross the railway (taking care not to be mown down by a train) and head once again towards the Anglian Water buildings to pick up the footpath that leads back to your car.

Nature lovers will want to take the section of nature trail up the west shore of the pit opposite the Anglian Water buildings since it is particularly rich in bird life and plants.

Walk 7
KING'S COLLEGE CHAPEL
CAMBRIDGESHIRE
7 or 2½ miles

This walk allows you to sneak up behind the Cambridge colleges with no intervening town to mar the impact of arriving at the most spectacular view of the most famous building in one of the world's great universities. Viewed from the Backs, across the river, King's College Chapel presents a gracious exterior which is surpassed only by the breathtaking interior with its Rubens painting and fan tracery described by Wordsworth as 'the branching roof self-poised, and scooped into ten thousand cells'.

A hundred years after Wordsworth wrote his Ecclesiastical Sonnets, another poet was declaring his affection for a small village some two miles from Cambridge.

'And Cambridgeshire, of all England
The shire for men who understand;
And of that district I prefer
The lovely hamlet Grantchester'

Rupert Brooke's popular poem *The Old Vicarage, Grantchester* has encouraged the village to remain lovely, and it is a natural starting place for the walk into Cambridge and Brooke's old college.

Park along Grantchester's main street or at the Rupert Brooke pub if you're planning a celebratory end to the walk. Just along the road and on the right is the beginning of the public footpath through the water meadows. This joins the main path to Cambridge which is paved (though generously covered in cowpats) all the way. You can leave the path and

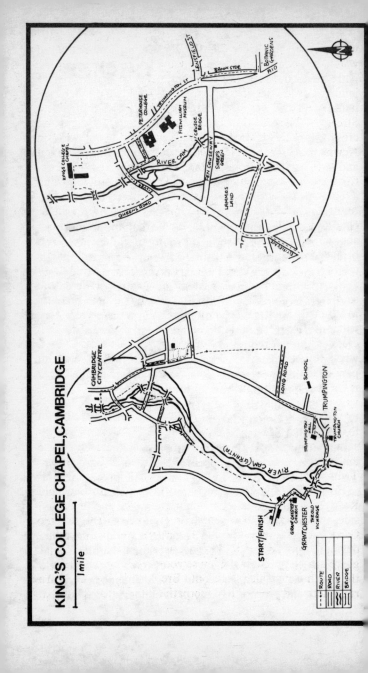

KING'S COLLEGE CHAPEL, CAMBRIDGE

1 mile

•-•-•	Route
▦	Road
≈	River
⌓	Bridge

KING'S COLLEGE CHAPEL

PETERHOUSE COLLEGE

TRUMPINGTON ST

FITZWILLIAM MUSEUM

CRUSOE BRIDGE

BROOK SIDE

LENSFIELD ST

BOTANIC GARDENS

A10

RIVER CAM

FEN CAUSEWAY

SHEEP'S GREEN

LAMMAS LAND

QUEEN'S ROAD

CAMBRIDGE CITY CENTRE

LONG ROAD

SCHOOL

TRUMPINGTON

TRUMPINGTON HALL

TRUMPINGTON CHURCH

RIVER CAM (GRANTA)

START/FINISH

GRANTCHESTER CHURCH

GRANTCHESTER

THE OLD VICARAGE

walk close to the River Cam (ready to jump any drains) to watch the undergraduates punt by and fall in. After a mile the path leaves the meadow and runs between hedges before joining a road. Bear left at a fork, down a line of Victorian houses (Eltisley Avenue) and left again into Grantchester Street. At the recreational area, Lammas Land, go right and cross the Mill Stream which once powered a watermill in Newnham village. These meadows are called Sheep's Green and have been common grazing land for hundreds of years. Cut diagonally across the meadow to the right, still following a footpath, and cross a small stream at a weir. Continue to a tunnel under Fen Causeway and cross the main river (Cam or Granta) and its Crusoe Island by a footbridge. You are now in another meadow, Coe Fen, and approaching another foot-bridge after which you turn left and follow the path to the city.

Peterhouse, the oldest college in existence anywhere (the south side dates from 1290), is on your right before you pass Mill Lane; take the little alley ahead, Laundress Lane. This will bring you out onto Silver Street where you turn left, crossing the river, and then right just past Queen's College where a footpath takes you to Queen's Road. Follow the path parallel to the road and the Backs entrance to King's College is the next possible turning to the right.

It is most unlikely that King's will be all you will wish to see of Cambridge. If you choose to linger, it is useful to know that there is a bus service from Cambridge bus station to Grantchester from Monday to Saturday. The longer route back for walkers is via the Botanic Gardens and Trumpington.

Follow Trumpington Street to its junction with Lensfield Road, turn left and immediately right to the end of Brook-side, a most attractive lane. The entrance to the Botanic Gardens is almost opposite. The gardens are open on week-days and summer Sunday afternoons; a good map and colour guide can be purchased. Choose your own route, but exit at the South Gate which leads onto Brooklands Avenue. Turn right here and proceed to a footpath on the left, signposted.

King's College Chapel from the Backs

This very pleasant path follows Hobson's Conduit (Thomas Hobson is, though, more famous for his Choice) near allotments, then through a spinney to Clare College sports ground. The path crosses a bridge to the left and skirts a large field to reach Long Road.

Here you turn right and walk along the footpath beside the road – uninspiring except for a very old milestone – until you reach the main road where you turn left. Half a mile on you'll see the war memorial and the entrance to Trumpington Hall on the right. Cross this busy road where you can and enter the main Hall drive to join a public footpath to the church.

The memorial brass to Sir Roger de Trumpington is the second oldest in England, dating from 1289, and is a mouth-watering sight to any brass-rubbing enthusiast. Beautifully preserved and protected by glass, it makes a visit to this little church well worthwhile. On leaving the church turn left down Church Lane and follow its meanderings to Grant-chester. If you take the duck-frequented riverside path on the right by the second bridge you will come out by Rupert Brooke's Old Vicarage and the Orchard Tea Gardens, where, no doubt, honey is still served. To maintain the Brooke feeling, of course, time your arrival at the church for ten to three!

Walk 8
CLEY-NEXT-THE-SEA
NORFOLK
5½ or 3½ miles

Glandford and Cley are two places of such interest that it was difficult to decide which should be the objective. I've settled on Cley, mainly because there is nowhere in Glandford to buy refreshments. If that isn't important to you, you could reverse the route described here, parking at the bottom of Old Woman's Lane. This double-ended walk is an ideal off-season choice since all the attractions are open throughout the year, and much of the walking is along country lanes.

Cley (pronounced Cly)-next-the-Sea should really be renamed Cley-over-a-mile-from-the-Sea since land reclamation in the seventeenth century caused the river to silt up and the village's prosperity as a major port was lost. Cley retains much charm, and one striking monument to its former splendour is the church of St Margaret's, one of the finest in Norfolk. This magnificent building of cathedral proportions gives an indication of Cley's early wealth, though the Black Death brought a halt to construction before the planned west tower could be built. There is much of interest inside, and a marvellously well-preserved brick table tomb in the churchyard commemorates one James Greeve who, in 1676, assisted in 'ye burning of ye Shipps in ye Port of Tripoly. . . ' and was 'presented with A Medal of Gold by King Charles ye 2nd'.

Our starting point, Glandford, is really a monument to one man, Sir Alfred Jodrell, the epitome of a Victorian benefactor. If you approach this, his model village with its Dutch-

CLEY-NEXT-THE-SEA

1 mile

BIRD SANCTUARY

PUBLIC HIDE
(BIRD WATCHING)

A149

WINDMILL

CLEY-NEXT
THE-SEA

A149

CHURCH LANE

OLD WOMAN'S LANE

RIVER GLAVEN

ST. MARGARET'S
CHURCH

SHORT ROUTE

CLEY
GREEN

BRIDGEFOOT
LANE

B1156

WIVETON

HAMMER
HILL

LAVENDER
HILL

HURDLE LANE

MILL

FORD

GLANDFORD

B1156

MUSEUM
GLANDFORD CHURCH

START/FINISH

N

---·--	ROUTE
=====	ROAD
~~	RIVER OR STREAM
⌒⌒⌒	BRIDGE
∴∴∴	HEATH
⊥⊥⊥	MARSH
⊥⊤	FIELD BOUNDARY

gabled houses, down the B1156 from Holt you will get a glimpse of Bayfield Hall, his stately home. You can park near St Martin's Church, rebuilt from ruins by Sir Alfred as a memorial to his mother. He crammed the tiny interior with all that is typical of East Anglian churches. There is a seven sacrament font, elaborate wood carving, gorgeous stained glass windows, a marble angel in memory of his mother, and a carved bench end in memory of his dog. The dog's dinner dish (silver, of course) is still used as an offertory plate at services. The church bells play hymn tunes every three hours, beginning at noon.

The Glandford Shell Museum has the same eccentric charm. There are not only hundreds of shells from all parts of the world, but also bits of mosaic purloined from Pompeii and an embroidered panel by a local fisherman-artist. The museum is open from Monday to Thursday 10am to 12.30pm, and 2pm to 4.30pm, on Fridays and Saturdays in the afternoon only, and is closed on Sundays.

Cross the River Glaven via the footbridge, but pause to consider that this now lazy brook was once tidal and navigable right up to this point. The converted mill you see downstream was one of 16 powered by the river. Continue straight ahead up Hurdle Lane – quite a steep climb but with lovely views – until you reach two public footpath signs where the road curves right; take the one to the left. Skirt a field and find a gap through the corner of the overgrown hedge into the next field. Follow the path steeply uphill through an ash grove and emerge high up on Lavender Hill with superb views across to Cley and Wiveton churches. The view is even better from the heathland of Hammer Hill on your right. The path now drops down and crosses Bridgefoot Lane, continuing as a track which brings you out on to a road. Here you turn left.

If you wish to follow the shorter route, continue straight along this road, passing Old Woman's Lane on the right, and you will soon come to Newgate Green, the Three Swallows pub and the fourteenth-century church of St Margaret's. This church, which now seems isolated from the rest of the

Windmill at Cley-next-the-Sea

village, was once in the centre, but the silting of the river and
a disastrous fire in 1612 caused the village to be rebuilt nearly
a mile to the north, by the present marshes.

By following Old Woman's Lane you can extend your walk
to this area. Just as you meet the main road turn left along a
narrow lane and follow the footpath to the right of the house
at the end. This brings you out onto the A149 opposite the
Beach Road. Follow the Beach Road and as it curves to the
right look out for a small footbridge across the ditch and up
onto the dyke path, followed to the left. This is a very
pleasant walk with fine views across the salt marshes towards
the windmill which is approached via a series of steps. The

path skirts the mill and follows the River Glaven to emerge by the George Inn.

You are now on the western outskirts of the village. Turn left and follow the main road to a shop on the right, 'Whalebone of Cley', so-called because around the original windows were whale jawbones. Its local name, Knucklebone House, is more descriptive, for in the cornices are set a variety of animal bones – vertebrae, knuckles and teeth. Up the side is a hollyhock-lined alley leading to Church Lane. As you would expect, this brings you to the church. Having visited this, take the footpath across the graveyard to Newgate Green, turn left and follow the narrow winding road leading back to Glandford, about a mile away.

Walk 9
FELBRIGG HALL
NORFOLK
4 or 2½ miles

Felbrigg Hall, about three miles south of Cromer, is the focus of this walk commemorating the de Felbrigg family who were lords of the manor in the fifteenth century. Sir Simon de Felbrigg was probably responsible not only for rebuilding most of the parish church of St Margaret's, which stands within the grounds, but also for the major alterations of the round-towered church at Aylmerton. Sir Simon became standard-bearer to King Richard II in 1395, a position which no doubt provided some useful cash for church building.

Our walk takes in these two churches as well as the magnificent Felbrigg Hall which was completely rebuilt by the successor of the de Felbriggs, the Wyndham family, who acquired the property in the mid-fifteenth century. The south front of the hall was built in 1620 by Sir John Wyndham, with a west wing added by his grandson William in 1686. The house has a lavish collection of eighteenth-century furniture and paintings and is open from April to October, 2pm – 6pm, Mondays, Wednesdays, Thursdays and weekends. The tea room and shop also stay open from 11am – 4pm from the end of October until just before Christmas.

In addition to the hall itself, don't miss the Orangery and walled garden with its eighteenth-century dovecot. The old kitchen, complete with seventeenth-century charcoal stove and set of shiny copper saucepans, has been turned into a very pleasant restaurant.

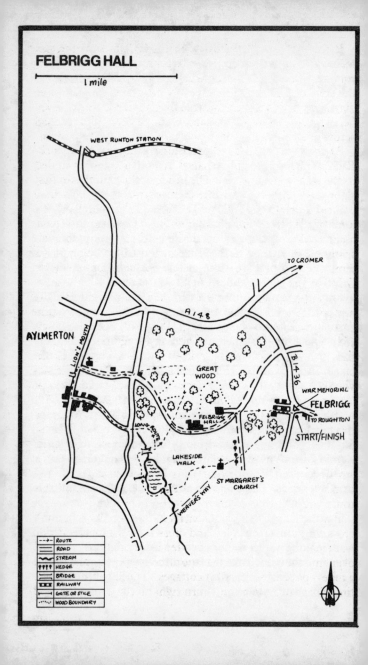

If driving, park at Felbrigg on the B1436, near the war memorial, and take the lower track past flint and brick cottages to a signpost for the Weaver's Way. The path follows the edge of a field and emerges by a larger field. Continue diagonally towards a line of trees that borders a track. From here the church of St Margaret's can be seen, and reached across a field of sugar beet.

At the church, note the precision of the flint flushwork. Each stone has been split, shaped in a square, and set so that its flat side faces outwards. The inside of the church is at first sight unimpressive, with the eighteenth-century box pews painted a dreary 'hospital beige'. It is the memorials to the lords of the manor that make this church special: under the mats in the aisle and by the altar are a series of brasses spanning two and a half centuries, the oldest being of Sir Simon de Felbrigg. There are also Wyndham monuments by Grinling Gibbons and Nollekens.

On leaving the churchyard turn left and cross a stile. Do not continue to the Weaver's Way sign ahead, but turn right and follow the field fence around. You will notice that this route is marked 'Lakeside Walk'. Across another stile you'll pass a short stretch of flint wall, then, as you approach the lake, an equally short red brick wall. Cross a narrow stile and you'll be at the lake's edge. Here you may see large flocks of Canada geese, duck, coot, moorhen and other waterfowl.

Continue along the path as it follows the left-hand shore of the lake and cross a stile into parkland dotted with trees. Skirt the edge of this pasture to another stile and turn sharp right across a bridge. Look out for herons fishing in the little stream here. The path now runs between two fences and brings you over a stile and through a copse. If you take this route you will emerge just below Felbrigg Hall.

For the longer walk which visits Aylmerton church, don't cross the stile but turn left and cross the park to a red brick wall, looking out for a short wooden ladder that will take you over onto the road. Take the lane directly opposite and in half a mile – passing typical flint cottages – you'll go through the tiny village of Aylmerton. Turn right on the T-junction and

Felbrigg Hall

the round tower of Aylmerton church can be seen ahead of you. This church stood in Saxon times but has been much restored. Round towers are relatively common in East Anglia where the local building material, flint, lends itself to this design, for no corner stones are needed. The inside is pleasant enought, but it is the graveyard that is of chief interest here. There are some very old headstones in excellent condition (one dated 1753), and, in spring and summer, an abundance of wild flowers. Fifty species have been recorded here, and the graveyard is registered with the Norfolk Naturalists' Conservation Scheme.

The route back to Felbrigg is down the dirt track by the church. At the lodge gates you can either proceed directly to the hall or take a longer route through the lovely Great Wood. The entrance to the latter is just to the left of the Lodge house. Follow the track through woods, bearing right at forks, and you will come out at the picnic area furnished with tables. Turn left and in a few minutes you will arrive at the house.

To return to the car, turn left from the Hall, past the garden, and follow the drive up to the junction with the track to the farm buildings. A clear footpath runs across a field, uphill, and will bring you out at the original Weaver's Way signpost.

Walk 10
HOW HILL GARDENS
NORFOLK
5½ miles

How Hill is an attractive Edwardian house built above some carefully designed and very beautiful gardens. The name comes from the Viking word for High Place, and it was its location on a hillside overlooking the river which first attracted its architect, Edward Boardman, at the end of the last century. In the course of designing the estate he planted 70,000 trees.

One of How Hill's attractions for jungle enthusiasts is the Carr Woodland, a dense swampy area of alder, willow and birch. A Visitor Centre and Nature Walk are being established which will help you understand and appreciate this unique 'Broadland in microcosm', but since the house is now a residential centre for field studies, the grounds are not always open. You should be able to visit the formal gardens on most Sundays in the summer, and the famous water gardens more often. Ring St Benets (069262) 555 for current information.

The walk begins in Ludham, an attractive Broads village with a particularly interesting church. When How Hill is closed Ludham makes an equally appealing destination, so the walk can be done in reverse. Either way you will enjoy some typical Broads scenery.

Ludham is accessible by bus from Norwich or Yarmouth or by car on the A1062. Before starting your walk, take a look at the church of St Catherine. This particular saint suffered martyrdom on a spiked wheel and the wheel emblem is cleverly worked into the roof of the fourteenth-/fifteenth-

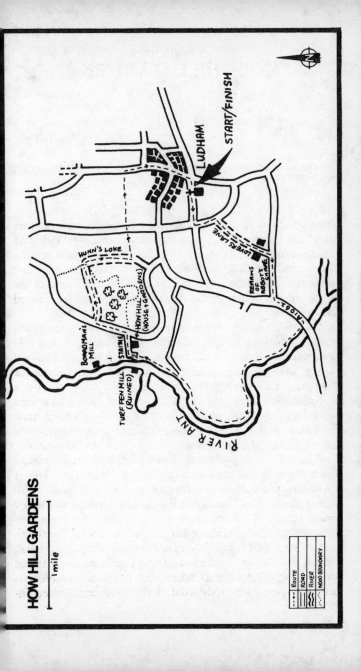

HOW HILL GARDENS

1 mile

- **ROUTE**
- **ROAD**
- **RIVER**
- **WOOD BOUNDARY**

LUDHAM

START/FINISH

HUNN'S LOKE

BOARDMAN'S MILL

TURF FEN MILL (RUINED)

STAITHE

HOW HILL (HOUSE + GARDENS)

LOWER LANE

REMAINS OF ABBOTS CHAPEL

A1062

RIVER ANT

N

century church. There is an interesting carved font, but the pride of the church is the painted rood screen separating the nave from the choir. Rood means a crucifix, and these were traditionally situated above the rood screen, but most were destroyed during the Reformation as symbols of Catholicism. The screen at Ludham has some lovely paintings, restored to their former glory a few years ago. They depict some unusual saints: St Walstan, patron of farming, and St Appolonia, patron of dentists (appropriately holding a drawn tooth), among others.

Apart from its paintings, the screen is particularly interesting for its tympanum (above the screen) which on one side shows a crucifixion scene and on the other the coat of arms of Queen Elizabeth I. Here is an indication of the swing of the sixteenth-century religious pendulum between the Protestant and Catholic faiths. First the Catholic-inspired screen paintings were defaced in the reign of Edward VI, then the tympanum crucifixion was hastily painted by a local artist when Queen Mary Tudor, a Catholic, came to the throne, but when Elizabeth was crowned this had to be replaced by her coat of arms. Finally, both were hidden from Cromwell's men and only came to light in 1879. All this is speculation, but it does provide a neat illustration of the problems besetting rural churchmen in those days.

On leaving the church turn left along the main road and then left again at the crossroads after a quarter of a mile. This is Lovers Lane. Go right at the fork and follow a green lane to a farm. The great brick barn on the right incorporates the remains of the private chapel of the Abbot of St Benet's. Turn right at the road and then left on the main road to Ludham Bridge. A footpath runs along the east bank of the River Ant to How Hill, with views of boats, marsh and water birds – typical broadlands scenes. After one and a half miles the path leaves the river, joining a track which leads back to Ludham. Don't take this track, but turn left along a bank which brings you through marshes and back to the river opposite the derelict Turf Fen wind pump. Continue following the river bank to the staithe (a local word meaning

Norfolk Broads scene

landing place). How Hill is the thatched house along the path uphill to the right.

There is another windmill, this time in good working order, just upstream from the staithe. Boardman's Mill, an open-framed timber tressle windpump, can be visited at any time of the year.

To return to Ludham, continue along the path to the road and another derelict windmill (being restored), turn left and head uphill before taking the green lane leading off to the right opposite a white house. This bridleway runs beside an orchard, then veers left to meet a track known as Hunn's Loke. Go right here, following the edge of two fields before turning away from the hedge of the green lane and striking across the field to the left. This right of way is none too clear, but you should arrive on the surfaced road, across which is a clearer bridleway running along the edge of a field to the road back to Ludham.

There are various ways of shortening this walk by missing out the long stretch of river part and joining the Ant by the marshes (see map).

Walk 11
BANHAM ZOO
NORFOLK
4½ or 3 miles

Banham Zoo was started in a small way in 1968 to provide additional entertainment for the shoppers buying vegetables in the farm store opposite. It is now a thriving and well-run zoo with an excellent selection of monkeys and other primates, including tiny toy-like marmosets and tamarins. Among the larger monkeys are Diana – a spider monkey born on a certain royal wedding day and hand-reared, now re-introduced to her family – and some chimpanzees who have devised an effective method of getting their own back on the staring public, judging by the warning 'Stand clear. The chimps could throw material of an objectionable nature!'

Before starting your Banham walk it's worth driving to Quidenham for the scenery around this old estate is most attractive. The hall is now a Carmelite monastery, not open to the public, but do visit the Saxon church which has a round tower.

The zoo lies to the west of Banham village on the B1113, and the walk begins on this rather busy road just outside Kenninghall. It's easiest to approach from Banham since the parking places are then on the left side of the road. Look for a slip road by a series of new houses culminating in some huge buildings used for chicken rearing. The footpath is across the road from the first house. This footpath is not signposted but is a well defined track across fields with a conspicuous notice requesting that dogs be kept on leads. This track brings you to Kenninghall Fen along which runs a very pleasant path.

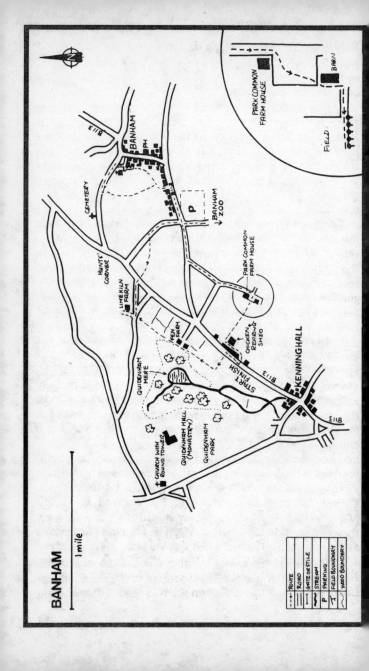

Follow this then turn right to pass marshland and then a pond (gravel pit). This area is excellent for waterfowl; if you go quietly you should see a good variety of duck as well as coot and moorhen.

The path continues past rough marshy grassland until you reach the edge of a wood and some farm buildings – Fen Farm. Here you go right, along the fence, and through a gate into the farm yard then left to continue along the path through a narrow grassy strip with a few houses on your right and woods on the left – a most attractive area. Keep following the hedge on your right and you will arrive at the lane opposite Limekiln Farm.

Turn right here and then left at the fork to the road junction. A bridleway runs down the track on the opposite side of the road. In fact it runs along the edge of the field to the right, but it's easier to follow the track to a rest home for rusting farm machinery then cross into the field when the going is easier. Skirt the edge of this large field, cross into the next one and continue straight across to the road. By turning right here you'll soon be on the main road opposite the zoo.

Before returning to the car you may want to take a look at Banham village which has a pretty little green with some attractive houses. Walk along the main road towards the village and look out for a footpath leading between houses about 200 yards along on the left. This leads by gardens on the right and (mostly) fields on the left, past your return footpath signposted off left to Hunt's Corner, until you emerge into Church Lane. The church interior is pleasant, if not spectacular, and has an effigy of a distinguished-looking fourteenth-century knight.

Take the lane closest to the church which leads to Hunt's Corner, and look out for a footpath on the left across a stile, just after the road crosses the stream. Go straight across, through a gap in the hedge to the next cow field, and head towards its left-hand corner to join the village footpath.

To return to the car you can either retrace your steps along Kenninghall Fen (the prettiest route) or take Park Common Lane, a quarter of a mile down the main road. (There is no

Banham Zoo

footpath by the road, so take care).

Park Common Lane, passing through a huge arable area known as Park Common, is a surfaced road with a minimum of traffic and a generous amount of grass growing down the middle. It leads to a few houses and the huge sheds of a chicken rearing unit. At Park Common Farmhouse turn right, across the yard, past a barn on your left, and pick up a track that leads to a field. The public right of way follows the edge of this field, bringing you out onto a grassy track by more chicken sheds. Turn left here, past a propane gas tank on your right, and on to the road where you parked your car.

Walk 12
BLYTHBURGH CHURCH
SUFFOLK
4 miles

Blythburgh Church – popularly known as the Cathedral of the Marshes – is considered to be one of the finest in East Anglia and is famous for its lovely 'angel roof' where life-sized angels spread their wings across the central beam. Holy Trinity Church was begun in 1412 and the great edifice was slowly raised over the following 80 years. In a violent storm in 1577 the steeple crashed through the roof, and legend attributed this to the Devil in person, scorch marks on the north door being made by his fingers as he left. The steeple was never rebuilt.

It is a beautiful building both inside and out. Full of light from the huge clear windows, rather empty, with a lovely pink brick floor, a fifteenth-century pulpit and a painted rood screen. Most of the stained glass was destroyed when William Dowsing left orders for the destruction of '200 pictures'. These were the panels of saints and other figures in the windows, and statues, in niches, that the Cromwellians hated so much. Luckily, the tie-beam roof with its carved angels was too high for Dowsing's men and their axes to reach.

Walberswick is only three miles from Dunwich, so you can connect this walk circuit with that of Walk 13 by taking the Suffolk Coast Path to the south. It is clearly marked and passes through the Walberswick National Nature Reserve, full of marsh wildlife. Visit the informative Heritage Coast Centre in Walberswick where you can pick up a leaflet

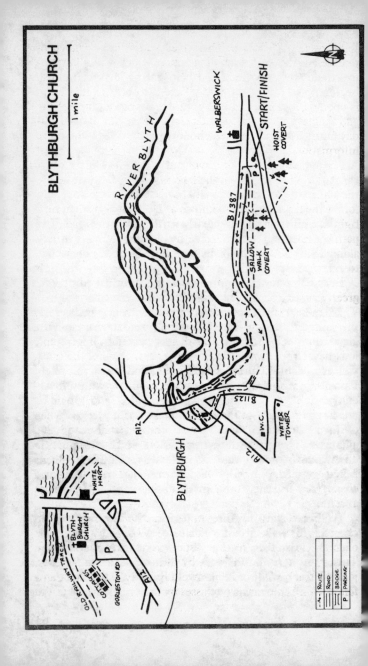

BLYTHBURGH CHURCH

1 mile

RIVER BLYTH

A12

B1125

A12

WATER TOWER

W.C.

BLYTHBURGH

B1387

SALLOW WALK COVERT

WALBERSWICK

START/FINISH

HOIST COVERT

BLYTH-BURGH CHURCH

WHITE HART

OLD RAILWAY TRACK

COTTAGES

GORLESTON RD

A12

P

---	ROUTE
---	ROAD
---	BRIDGE
P	PARKING

Walberswick Walksheet. This gives you a large choice of rambles in the area, including routes which will allow you to extend the walk described below to about seven miles, beginning at one of the two village car parks. The Centre is open daily (except Monday) in the afternoon during July and August, and on weekends from the Spring Bank Holiday until September. Telephone Ipswich 55801 for more information.

For our shorter circuit leave your car at the Hoist Covert car park half a mile down the lane that forks left just before the church as you leave Walberswick. Cross the road and follow the track by a wood known as Hoist Covert, then turn right at a junction and follow this path back to the road. The path continues on the other side and leads to a track running along Sallow Walk Covert. Bear right at the end of the woods to arrive at the B1387.

Turn left along the road and after about half a mile take a green lane on the right as the road makes a turn to the left. This bridlepath is very easy walking, along a wide track pleasantly lined with trees and bushes. Heather and harebells grow by the wayside, and further on are clumps of ferns and lots of different sorts of moss. Towards the end of the track you can see the church straight ahead through the trees. Passing by corn fields you'll see two World War 2 pillboxes on the right.

The bridle path comes out onto the B1125 opposite a group of new houses and a telephone box. Turn right along the road and pass a pretty but sadly dilapidated Methodist Chapel. Take the short road to the left: this meets the A12; cross and head for the church. This magnificent building and a small cluster of houses is all that is left of the busy medieval port and market town that once was Blythburgh.

To return, start from the car park and head away from the church up a dirt road (Gorleston Road) which goes past a row of cottages on the right. The last one is named 'Daisy Bank'. Turn right here, along a path by the side of the cottage and join the track of the old Southwold Railway. Turn right and follow along the track as it passes by the back gardens of the

Bench End carving, depicting 'Sloth' in Blythburgh Church

cottages on one side and the River Blyth on the other. Passing by the north end of the church, you get marvellous views of it rising up against the wide East Anglian skies. The path continues across the main road, behind a low white cottage.

After passing the helpful board-map, cross a stile and take the path ahead. On your right, The White Hart, an attractive inn which was once a courthouse, has a picnic area. The river and marsh are to the left. The path narrows, with marsh on either side for much of the way, and it can be very muddy and overgrown in the summer. It winds gently by the river through blackberries, broom and gorse.

After crossing two footbridges you'll see a bird-watching hide, through the reed beds on the left, which can be reached at low tide. Beyond the marshland and the blue-grey river, the feeding ground of many birds, weathered pines make a dark and jagged line on the horizon. Continue towards a stile, passing a stunted and twisted oak, the first of many such trees. Across a third footbridge the path opens out as it reaches high bracken-covered ground: a pleasant shady place for a summer picnic with lots of old trees for children to climb on or play under. A fallen tree makes a good place to sit and admire the view of Blythburgh village and its church across the marsh and, in summer, to smell the honeysuckle. The ground is sandy here and full of rabbit holes. Old timber embedded in the path is a reminder that this was the track of a single line railway, which must have been a delightful way to reach Southwold.

As the path continues, it leaves the marsh and passes through open, sandy land with bracken and stunted pine trees. The footpath now joins your earlier bridle path which leads ahead with a 'horse riders only' notice; to the right is a footpath. Either will take you to the road. Walk towards Walberswick, looking out for the bridle path to the right which leads across a field to the car park.

Walk 13
DUNWICH
SUFFOLK
6 miles

This delightful and varied walk takes you along a cliff, across a heather-clad common and through woods to a no-more town: Dunwich, once capital of East Anglia, whose early greatness was due to the sea and which ultimately was lost to the sea.

The recorded history of Dunwich goes back to 630 AD when St Felix brought Christianity to the Saxon town there, but there was probably a Roman settlement before that. For two centuries Dunwich was a centre for learning, and its then sheltered harbour made it England's second most important port, bringing its prosperity to a peak in the reign of Henry II. Then in 1528 came devastating floods; the River Blyth broke through the sandy spit that protected the harbour, and the gradual loss of the town through erosion began. Through the centuries the sea nibbled away at the cliffs, claiming its last building, All-Saints' Church, in 1919. It is said that the church bells still peal beneath the waves.

An excellent small museum chronicles the decline of the town and has a model of Dunwich in its prime; an inn selling Real Ale and some of the best fish and chips in East Anglia complete the attractions.

The walk begins in an area of outstanding natural beauty, Dunwich Common (or Heath), owned by the National Trust. Leave the B1125 at Westleton and follow the signs first to Dunwich and then to Minsmere. At the end of the road is a large (paying) car park. Walk to the cliff edge near

DUNWICH

1 mile

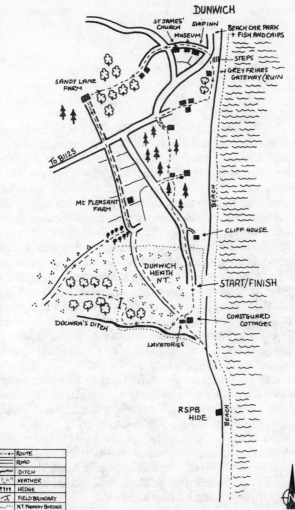

DUNWICH

St James' Church
Museum
Ship Inn
BEACH CAR PARK + FISH AND CHIPS
STEPS
GREY FRIARS GATEWAY (RUIN)

SANDY LANE FARM

To B1125

BEACH

Mt PLEASANT FARM

CLIFF HOUSE

DUNWICH HEATH N.T.

START/FINISH

DOCWRA'S DITCH

COASTGUARD COTTAGES

LAVATORIES

RSPB HIDE

BEACH

--+--	ROUTE
	ROAD
	DITCH
	HEATHER
	HEDGE
	FIELD BOUNDARY
	N.T. PROPERTY BORDER

the warden's hut and continue south along the heather-clad cliffs with spectacular views of the beach and sea far below. Half-way along there are steps leading to the sands or you can reach the beach near the coastguard cottages at the cliff's end. Continue along the shore for half a mile and you'll come to the RSPB hide, from which can be seen a large variety of birds.

From the coastguard cottages a broad track leads straight across the common, cutting nearly a mile off the walk described below. The prettier route, however, starts just past the lavatories where a faint path can be seen leading down through the bracken to Docwra's Ditch, dug as a fire-break but now stocked with fish. The little path follows this stream through high bracken (a good area for seeing reptiles) with a scattering of silver birch – a delightful walk. After about half a mile it curves round to the right and soon you'll come to an iron rail across a gate. Arrows indicate 'NT walk' to the right and 'East Bridge' to the left. Go left. This path takes you through heather and dwarf silver birch, then conifers leading to mixed deciduous woods.

Turn right on reaching a broad sandy track/bridle path which cuts across the heath. You are now surrounded by heather. Go over a gentle hill, with good views from the top, and the track suddenly becomes a narrow and rather over-grown path between hedges of blackthorn, elder, blackberry and gorse. You'll emerge at a loop of track which forms a crossroads with the alternative path from the coastguard cottages. Turn left along the track, past Mount Pleasant Farm and out onto the road. Take the track opposite, leading to Sandy Lane Farm, and turn right at the farm down a footpath (Sandy Lane) which was once an old road. This will take you to Dunwich, passing through pleasant woodland until you reach two cottages whose long drive brings you out onto the road by the church.

It's worth visiting this church, built on the site of an old leper hospital – the ruins remain – in the nineteenth century. Some of the treasures from All-Saints' church ended up here. Follow the signs to the beach and you'll pass a gift shop, the

Avocets at Dunwich

Ship Inn, and Dunwich car park and cafe. Before indulging, however, take a look at the museum which is on the right. It's open from 2pm to 4pm, May to September, on Tuesdays, Thursdays and weekends. In August it opens every day, and in March, April and October on weekends only. The museum can be visited at other times by appointment. Telephone Westleton 358.

To return to Minsmere and the Heath you can either walk along the beach or take a higher, more varied route. From the car park walk very briefly along the beach and then up the steps leading to the cliff walk. Follow the footpath signposted to Dunwich Church Lands. On the right of the path is the ruined Greyfriar's Gateway. Continue through sycamore then sharp right at a fence, under a concrete arch, and emerge at Greyfriars. There are some charming cottages here, with 'barley sugar' chimneys. A footpath on the left to Minsmere

Road takes you up a drive apparently to a private house, but the track continues to the right of the buildings, through mostly coniferous woods, past a house on the left and crosses a track. Continue following the path to the road. Turn left and arrive back at your car after about half a mile.

If you want to shorten the first part of this walk, go right at the gate leading to East Bridge, then left (following sign to 'NT Walk') on the main Heath track. Follow this uphill by domes of heather, keeping an eye out for a gate (single rail) on the left. This takes you to the track leading to Mount Pleasant farm.

(To connect this walk with the previous one, see description for Walk 12.)

Walk 14
JACOB'S FARM, LAXFIELD
SUFFOLK
4½ miles

Laxfield lies on the B1117, about six miles north of Framlingham in East Suffolk. A pretty little village in typical Suffolk farming country, it offers two main attractions: the Guildhall Museum and Jacob's Farm Children's Museum with a pleasant walk between the two.

The farm began its life some 400 years ago as Jacob's Hall, and the present owners have recently turned it into a museum of childhood and a smallholding specialising in rare breeds. Greeted at the gate by a large and bouncy Newfoundland dog, you can scratch the snout of Bluebell and Clover, the Gloucester Old Spot pigs, and watch the happy munchings of Southdown and Jacob sheep and Dexter cows.

A moat, destroyed in parts by the road, runs round the farm – a common feature of farms in East Anglia. Clay was needed for house-building and moats were a useful by-product. They drained the land in the winter and provided extra water in the summer. Livestock was kept coralled and watered, safe from wolves or thieves.

The museum itself has a collection of dolls, teddy bears, and other toys. There is also a reconstructed Victorian schoolroom and old style kitchen where teas are served. When the old chimney of this kitchen was being repaired, they found evidence of witchcraft: a bag containing, among other things, a dried mouse and a bird's wing.

Jacob's Farm is open every day in the school holidays, from 10am to 5pm, and on Tuesdays, Thursdays and

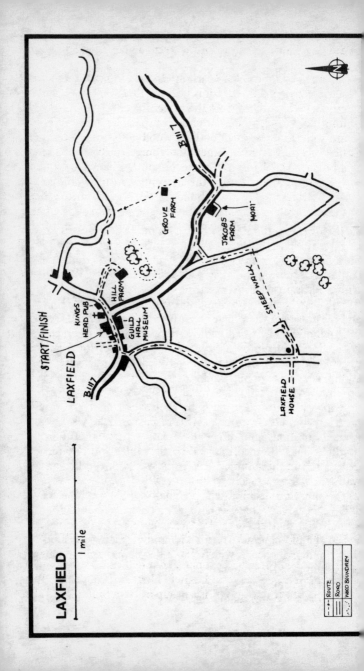

Sundays during the rest of the year. There is an admission fee.

You should be able to park in Laxfield village, and before setting out on your walk it is well worth visiting the church, most of which dates from the fifteenth century. The nave is unusually wide, giving the church a spacious interior. There are some fine carvings both in wood and stone (note particularly the Seven Sacrament font, one of the best of its kind) all defaced by Cromwell's henchman, William Dowsing.

Opposite the church is the sixteenth-century Guildhall, a fine half-timbered brick building. It houses an excellent museum relating to the domestic and working life of the village at the turn of the century. There are several rooms including a little kitchen and an old style privy, a display of wearing apparel, farm implements, household utensils, toys, and even an active beehive. The museum is open from 2pm to 5pm at weekends from Spring Bank Holiday until the end of September, and at other times by appointment: telephone Ubbeston 584/218. There is no admission charge, so please be generous with your donations.

On leaving the museum turn left. Nearby is the Baptist church and a memorial to John Noyes who was burned at the stake in the reign of Queen Mary for his Protestant faith. Legend has it that he was brought back to his home village to meet his death but no fire could be found with which to light the faggots piled around the stake. All the villagers had extinguished their household fires – something one avoided doing before the invention of matches. It was only after a long search that they found a fire tended by an old lady who had not realised what was going on. John Noyes was a cobbler, and a further legend has it that his foot and shoe never burned.

The walk to Jacob's Farm takes you further down the road to the war memorial where you turn left and left again down Mill Road. These lanes carry very little traffic so it's a pleasant walk for the next one and a half miles when you'll pass the leafy driveway of Laxfield House on your right. Just beyond this, on your left, is a group of farm buildings. Take

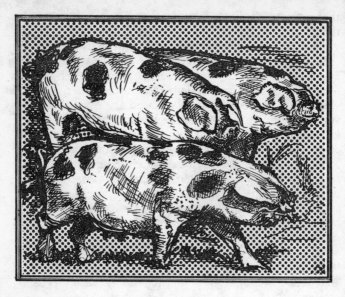

Gloucester Old Spot pigs

the track that runs between them and through the fields. This is the Sheep Walk (or Sheepdip Walk from the dipping ditch at the east end) which was used for taking animals to market. Originally it ran between hedges, but though most of these have been grubbed up it's still easy to follow (though not an official right of way: please respect the landowner's kind permission to cross). Turn left at the lane then, after a quarter of a mile, right and right again onto the B1117. Jacob's Farm is on the right, shortly after the road makes a turn to the right. This road carries a fair bit of traffic, so take care.

After visiting the farm, the first quarter mile of the walk back to Laxfield is along the B1117 (turn right on leaving the farm yard). Soon after the road makes a sharp turn to the left you will see a sign to Ubbeston and a track leading off to the left alongside a field. Officially this public footpath leaves the track after the first field and takes you across farm land to the left of Grove Farm. However the owner kindly allows walkers to continue along the track and through the farm (where bed and breakfast is available), then down its drive to a lane. Turn left here and left again at a wooden public footpath sign crossing a little plank bridge.

Laxfield church is now visible ahead and is your guide as you skirt around the field to the left and join a lane which leads to Hill Farm. Keep going straight ahead and you'll come out just below Laxfield church and the Kings Head. This pub has remained unchanged for hundreds of years and makes a fitting end to your day. There is no bar, but the proprietor will seat you next to the old fireplace with its ancient cooking apparatus and serve you local cider and home-made meals. There is a second pub, also serving Real Ale and meals, on the main road.

Walk 15
WOODBRIDGE TIDE MILL
SUFFOLK
8 or 7 miles

The unique tide mill at Woodbridge was functioning until 1956 and used the force of the tide to grind corn. It has now been beautifully restored and is open to the public from 11am to 1pm, and 2.30pm to 5pm daily, July to September, on weekends in June and October, and also during the Easter holiday. A little booklet is available which gives clear explanations of all the machinery so that even children can understand this effective harnessing of natural energy. On summer weekends you can take the ferry to Sutton Hoo from near the tide mill – an enjoyable extension.

One of Suffolk's most attractive towns, Woodbridge lies on the River Deben. You begin at Martlesham, on the southern outskirts of Woodbridge off the A12 from Ipswich. If approaching from Woodbridge take the prominent fork on the left at Crown Point. From Ipswich it's easier to take the A1093 towards Felixstowe and then left and left again. There is a broad verge with picnic spots and plenty of room for parking.

A path runs through the woods to the south of Mill Lane, though the public footpath sign has almost disappeared. Follow this for half a mile through mixed deciduous trees and emerge into a lane opposite a corn field. A footpath crosses this field but it is easier to turn left and follow the road, taking the first turning to the right. The Ordnance Survey map shows the footpath crossing this road but it has been diverted. The new path starts a little way beyond the one

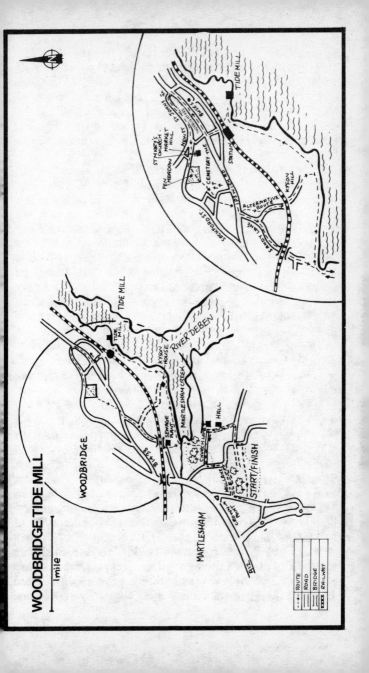

across the cornfield, leading off to the left along the headland of a field to Hall Farm Cottage and then Martlesham Hall where it skirts Church Lane to emerge opposite the footpath signposted to Martlesham Creek. This takes you downhill through woods, across a brook, and over another stile to the creek, which is really an arm of the Deben estuary. This is a great place for bird watchers as the path crosses a dyke between the marshlands.

After crossing a sluice, veer round to the right keeping close to the water (don't take the path straight ahead leading to the sewage plant). This path is rather faint and rough in places but soon broadens as it approaches the main river. At Kyson Point it curves round to the left, passing some boats and a boat shed (this part may be wet underfoot at high tide), and continues along the River Deben. The white tide mill will now be visible in the distance. The path soon leaves the river (don't be tempted to continue to hug the bank – it's very muddy) and goes up towards Kyson Hill. At Kyson House drop down to the river again and follow the asphalt path to a marina and the tide mill.

The next part of the walk shows you some of the most picturesque streets of Woodbridge, but the whole town is so interesting that a more extensive tour is advised. From the tide mill take the track across the railway line to Quayside, turn left, then right up Quay Street. Take the first right along The Thoroughfare and left up St John's Street which leads to New Street – new in the late Middle Ages. Here is an inn which was once a seventeenth-century weighhouse or steel-yard. The machine that weighed cart loads, housed in a little wooden extension, still overhangs the road. Beyond New Street is the famous Market Hill and its Elizabethan Shire Hall with Dutch style gables, added later, a reminder of the closeness of Holland to East Anglia. Nearby is the equally old St Mary's Church.

Seckford Street, leading from Market Hill, is named after the town's chief benefactor, Thomas Seckford, whose tomb is in St Mary's. The elegant Seckford almshouses, now a hospital, are further down the road. We are now opposite a

Woodbridge Tide Mill

piece of open common known as Fen Meadow. Cross this, going uphill, to Fen Walk which runs past the cemetery; you will see some graves on the right-hand side. Continue to the road, keeping the main cemetery on your left, cross Warren Hill Road and take the alley opposite. At the end of the path a series of steps lead to Ipswich Road where you turn right and immediately left down Sandy Lane.

The shortest route back to the car is to continue along the road and under the railway bridge, picking up the path to Martlesham Creek by the sewage works. Alternatively, take the surfaced path that starts on the left at the beginning of Sandy Lane, by a telephone box, and runs past woods on the left before meeting a road. Continue in the same direction, past the Broomheath (an open space with good views), over the railway, and join the river path at Kyson Hill.

Retrace your earlier steps along the head of the creek and through the woods, then turn right on Church Lane. Turn left at the T-junction then right down Mill Lane, the track which forms the bar of the next T-junction. This will bring you out near your car.

The less energetic can halve the distance of this walk by taking a bus back from Woodbridge to Martlesham; you can get off at Crown Point.

People without a car can start the walk in Woodbridge, accessible by bus or train from Ipswich.

Walk 16
LAVENHAM
SUFFOLK
2½ miles

This gem of a walk to Suffolk's loveliest wool town is short
and easy enough to be suitable for grannies and young
children. An ideal off-season walk, it is probably best
avoided on bank holidays or in the height of the summer
when the town is bursting with visitors.

The popular name 'wool town' is a misnomer, since
Lavenham and its neighbours gained prosperity from all
types of manufactured cloth, including horsehair and even
coconut matting. It was wool, however, in its woven and
unwoven form, that made this town so prosperous in Tudor
times. Such was its importance that a contemporary Flemish
map of Europe in Antwerp museum shows Lavenham as one
of England's principal towns.

As was customary in those days, the wealth was used to
build as large and fine a church as possible. No doubt there
was some rivalry with nearby towns in building for the glory
of God. In the inevitable comparison between Lavenham and
Long Melford, the latter wins on size but Lavenham has the
highest tower – 141 feet. This tower was never completed,
though, and there are indications that battlements and
turrets were planned. Legend has it that the architect died
in a fall from the tower and it would have been unlucky to
finish it.

Begin the walk by parking by the old railway bridge on
Bridge Street Road, west of Lavenham, and walk along the
road past Slough Farm. This approach gives you a wonderful

LAVENHAM

1 mile

A1141

LAVENHAM

A. MARKET PLACE
B. BOWLTON ST.
C. GUILDHALL

SHILLING ST.

WATER STREET

WI MAP OF LAVENHAM

HIGH ST

HALL RD

PARK ROAD

CHURCH STREET

WALK

LAVENHAM

DISUSED RAILWAY

BASILDON HALL FARM

START/FINISH P

SLOUGH FARM

→ →	ROUTE
|||	ROAD
)(	BRIDGE
P	PARKING
⌃	FIELD BOUNDARY

view of the church tower thrusting up from the surrounding flatness. Keeping the tower in sight you turn left after about half a mile up a very well defined footpath across a field (mercifully – and unusually in East Anglia – the path has been ploughed around not ploughed up) and follow the hedge of the adjacent field to emerge on the outskirts of town at Hall Road. Turn right to the church.

Probably a Norman church originally stood here which was rebuilt between 1485 and 1525, mainly through the generosity of Thomas Spring III, a cloth merchant known as 'the great clothier', and John de Vere, thirteenth Earl of Oxford. Thomas Spring's donation might have been something of an act of repentance, for in 1508 he applied for, and received, a 'general pardon' from Henry VII for 'all murders, felonies, . . . rebellions, contempt, etc, also of all usurious contracts . . . corrupt covenants, etc, of illicit sales of cloth, wool, linen, and for non-payment of misdeeds in making cloth. . . ' The inside of the church is notable mainly for its fine wood carving, especially the fourteenth-century screen and tomb enclosures.

When you leave the church go round its north side and pick up a footpath which leads through a pleasant meadow near the site of the former Hall, residence of the de Vere family. It passes a small lake, surviving from medieval times, known as The Fishpond.

The path brings you out again on Hall Road and so on to the High Street. This, and other streets in Lavenham, has a children's story book quality; colourful timbered houses lean against each other in drunken fashion, their jetties overhanging the pavement. To see the best of this most perfect of English medieval towns, turn right along the High Street and then left along Water Street. At the east corner is an illustrated map of the town, donated by the Women's Institute. Water Street has many attractive buildings, including The Priory, De Vere House, and the Old Forge Bookshop. Descriptions of these and all the interesting buildings in Lavenham can be found in the booklet *A Walk around Lavenham* published by the Suffolk Preservation

Lavenham Church

Society, whose headquarters are in Little Hall, Market Place.

From Water Street take the third turning on the left up Shilling Street, crammed with interesting houses and leading to the old centre of town, the Market Place. Here is the splended Guildhall, another representation of the wealth of sixteenth-century Lavenham, where the merchants met for their wheeling and dealing in the cloth trade. Later it became the Town Hall, then a bridewell (prison), then successively a workhouse, almshouse and wool-store. It is now National Trust property and houses a small museum.

On the other side of the square from the Guildhall is the fifteenth-century Angel Hotel a good place for refreshments before walking back to the car. To the right of the hotel an alley takes you back to the High Street where you turn right. The way-marked Lavenham Walk begins just before the bridge and takes you down the old railway track, under Park

Road bridge, then between very English hedges of blackberry, blackthorn and hawthorn back to your car.

Walk 17
KENTWELL HALL
SUFFOLK
7or 5½ miles

There are two approaches to the fine 'wool town' of Long Melford with its many medieval buildings and splendid church, both making Kentwell Hall the objective. The shorter one is a circular route, and the other involves taking a bus (or arranging transport) to Lavenham.

Kentwell Hall is a splendid Elizabethan moated manor house, the owners of which use imaginative ideas to avoid this being just another stately home. You can watch the painstaking restoration work, for instance, and each year there is an event in the summer when everyone dresses up in Tudor fashion and talks in 'prithees' and 'good sirs'. The house and gardens are open from Easter to the end of September, on Wednesdays, Thursdays and Sundays from 2pm to 6pm, and weekends during the school holidays from 12pm to 6pm. Telephone (0787) 310207 for details. There is an admission charge.

The circular walk begins at Bridge Street, a collection of houses with a post office and pub – the Rose and Crown – on the A134 road to Bury St Edmunds. (A Youth Hostel at Alpheton, a mile to the north, provides a convenient centre from which to explore this area). Assuming you'll be thirsty on your return, you can leave your car in the pub car park. Cross the main road to the lane opposite. The public footpath begins, clearly signposted, across the road from an antique dealer. The broad track, probably an old road, follows the Chad Brook for much of its course into Long Melford. After

LONG MELFORD

1 mile

N

START (B)

LAVENHAM

B1071

A1141

DISMANTLED RAILWAY

PARADISE WOOD

LINERAGE WOOD

BRIDGE STREET

A134

CHAD BROOK

ALLOTMENTS

ROSE + CROWN PUB

START/ FINISH (A)

SHELTHORN WOOD

KENTWELL HALL

KILN FARM

RECTORY

HOLY TRINITY CHURCH

ROUTE (9)

LANGTON DRIFT

LODGE PARK

MELFORD HALL (N.T.)

P ROUTE (9)

LONG MELFORD

	ROUTE
	ROAD
	BROOK
	WOOD BOUNDARY
	FIELD BOUNDARY
	GATE

skirting a field the path runs between hedges of blackthorn, elder and hawthorn. Beyond the next field it makes a sharp right turn across an old bridge over the brook and continues to follow its right bank by the woods along the headland of a sloping field. The public footpath was ploughed up, making walking difficult, but may now have been reinstated.

At the end of the field the path enters an arm of Crabtree Wood where rough ground, nettles and burdock may impede your progress for a short distance before you join a good Forestry Commission track. Turn right here and follow the headland of a huge field, still skirting the woods, and pass the junction of the Lavenham Walk. The path is easy to follow from here as it continues to the end of the woods, then makes a right turn uphill towards Lodge Farm. The last part is along a surfaced track, Hare Drift, which leads to Melford High Street and a good pub, the Hare Inn.

Kentwell Hall's entrance is across the road, but first take a look at Holy Trinity Church, magnificently rebuilt in 1484 by the Clopton family, lords of the manor at Kentwell, when East Anglia was at the height of its prosperity from the wool trade. Norman Scarfe, author of the *Shell Guide* to this county, calls the church 'the supreme building in Suffolk'. The best view of its exterior is from the public footpath that leads off from the lower end of Kentwell Hall drive and circles the graveyard before bringing you out by the rectory.

The three-quarters of a mile-long approach to Kentwell Hall is lined with pollarded limes, planted in 1678, making a beautiful shady walk on a hot summer day. The entry to the courtyard of the house itself is dramatic; a bridge across the moat looks onto a brick maze in the design of a Tudor Rose. The lovely walled garden in the rear is designed to be viewed from one of the bedroom windows.

The footpath back to Bridge Street goes to the west of the hall around a paddock, and continues up a track to a junction. Continue ahead (the track here is straight and dull) until you come to Kiln Farm where you turn right, skirting a wood, pass a pheasant hatchery, and go along the edge of a field to the next wood, Ashen Grove. Here the path divides,

Holy Trinity Church, Long Melford

the left branch going through the wood and the other, which you take, keeping close to the south side of the wood and then crossing into the next field to walk alongside a small copse.

Care is needed to follow the next section as the path is not well defined. At the end of the copse bear slightly left towards the end of a short hedge. Turn left along this towards the farm, but at the ditch on the left turn right across the field, pass through an old gateway and down over the next field to the right end of a row of houses. Cross the road and continue down the right side of allotments before bearing right to the Rose and Crown.

The one-way walk from Lavenham is much easier than the circuit described above since it is simply a matter of following the old railway track, so you may prefer it providing you can arrange a lift or fit in with the bus times from

Long Melford to Lavenham. Check the schedule by phoning (0787) 227233.

The track begins at the north end of town and after passing under Bridge Street Road it goes through a nature conservation area, then past Lineage Wood to join the Chad Brook walk after two and a half miles. You can continue to Kentwell Hall or see more of Long Melford beforehand by turning left at Hare Drift and following Roydon Drift to Bull Lane. Turn right here and left at Bull Lane Farm to pick up the section of old railway track known as the Melford Walk.

This brings you out on the Sudbury Road at the southern end of town, so you can stroll up the long High Street and admire the many interesting houses on your way to Kentwell Hall which is on the left at the end of the village, past the church.

An excellent little guide to the most important buildings, *Along Melford*, can be purchased from the Historical and Archaeological Society in Bull Lane.

Walk 18
CONSTABLE'S WALK: FLATFORD MILL
SUFFOLK
7¼, 6½ or 4½ miles

Constable country is one of the major tourist attractions of East Anglia, and Flatford Mill its best-known scene. And scene it is, rather than museum, since the mill itself is not open to the public but is leased to the Field Studies Council by the National Trust. Nearby is Willy Lott's cottage, unchanged since it provided the background for the picture 'The Hay Wain'. The National Trust has acquired Bridge Cottage and restored it to house an exhibition showing Constable's working procedures. Bridge Cottage and its tea room is open from May to October.

A lovely riverside path follows the route taken by the young John Constable between school in Dedham and his home in Flatford Mill. Britain's first great landscape artist portrayed the west Suffolk countryside in a number of paintings. 'The Hay Wain', 'The Cornfield', 'The Valley of the Stour' and, of course, 'Flatford Mill' are all recognisable along this walk.

You begin in Dedham, which lies to the east of the A12, Colchester to Ipswich road. Just over the border in Essex, it is a charming village full of interesting places to visit. Another artist lived here: Sir Alfred Munnings, who painted horses. There's a permanent exhibition of his work at Castle House. Horse-lovers will also want to see the Dedham Vale Shire Horse Centre, and Americans will find the church particularly interesting for much of the restoration work was paid for by the people of Dedham in Massachusetts.

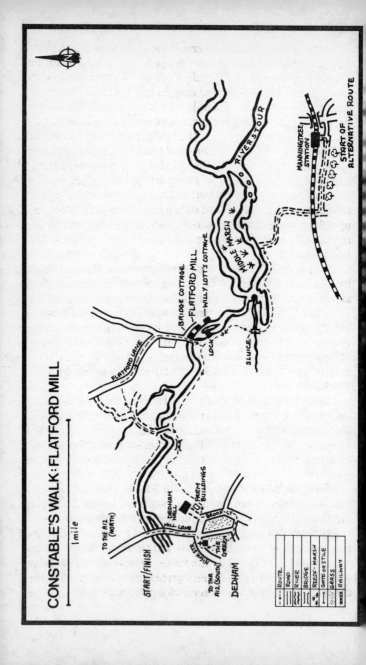

CONSTABLE'S WALK: FLATFORD MILL

1 mile

N

Leave your car at the riverside car park between the two bridges on Mill Lane. Cross the road, and to the left of the bridge is a low stile which takes you to the river. Follow its north bank, where weekend anglers fish for chub, for about half a mile, then cross a stile to a narrow path between a barbed wire fence and the river. The new bridge soon comes into view, an exact replica of the bridge painted by Constable in 'The Stour Valley'. The original one fell down in 1920 and was replaced in 1985 with the aid of the Manpower Services. Don't cross the bridge but swing left up the track, cross a small stream, and where two tracks cross follow the public footpath sign straight ahead over a stile. This path takes you uphill across pleasant meadowland with good views, to the road. Turn right here and go downhill to the car park and Flatford Mill.

To return to Dedham, cross the Stour over the footbridge by Flatford Mill and take the signposted public footpath along the south bank. This is a beautiful stretch of river; the path takes you by willow trees, swans, and a small herd of Highland cattle. After about a mile you cross a little concrete bridge over a ditch. Here the path leaves the river and is clearly marked as it crosses two fields and brings you out by a farm and then to Brook Street just by the entrance to Dedham Hall.

To see a bit more of Dedham before returning to your car, turn left and take the first narrow lane on your right past a half-timbered pink house, and cross the Green to the church. Opposite the church is Mill Lane. A tea shop is on the corner, or refreshments may be bought in the restaurant by the car park.

In winter, when the amenities of Flatford Mill are closed, you may prefer to start at the car park there so you can make Dedham the half-way point for rest and refreshments.

Flatford Mill is also accessible by public transport. Trains run, including Sundays, from Ipswich and Harwich to Manningtree. For the timetable telephone Colchester 392578. The walk from Manningtree station is interesting for the marshes and birdlife seen along the way, and can be

Dedham Lock and Mill, after John Constable

combined with the river walk to Dedham making a total of 7¼ miles. Take the track which leads from the entrance of the station by a white gate and runs parallel to the railway along a line of poplar trees. The track crosses under the railway and follows the edge of a field. After bending to the left it makes another turn to the right down a grassy track and over a stile. Here you meet the river and turn left.

The path takes you along a bank built to contain the river after the major flood of 1952. The sluice that forms part of the walk and now crosses mainly dry land was also built at this time. The River Stour is no longer tidal; in 1971 a sluice was built at Cattawade that controls the water flow downriver, allowing river water to flow down unimpeded but preventing tidal waters from flooding the countryside. You are now following the left of two arms of the river which embrace a reedy area known as Middle Marsh. This is a well-known spot for waterfowl, especially winter migrants; curlew, redshank, and snipe are often seen.

As you approach the sluice the path forks. Ignore the left one and continue straight ahead over a stile and across the sluice. Flatford Mill is at the end of the path.